YOUR FAITH

+

YOUR PHONE

A 30-DAY DEVOTIONAL

SUSAN B. ARICO

Cover and interior designs by Dara Dunn, Good Design Studios

ISBN (paperback) 9798418359322

www.susanbarico.com

For the ultimate communicator, the Word who
"became flesh and made his dwelling among us" (John 1:14)–
that our ways of connecting would be like his.

—

CONTENTS

INTRODUCTION

Our Phones and Presence:
God is with Us More Than Our Phones

Day 1: The Gift of Place   14
Day 2: The Present is Where God Sees Us   16
Day 3: The Present is Where God Makes Us Free   18
Day 4: We Walk with God in the Present Moment   20

What's So Great About Attention?
God Wants It; Phones Steal It

Day 5: Attention: "Not for Sale"?   24
Day 6: What We Look at, Listen to, and Actually Do   26
Day 7: In the Contest of Attention God Wins
       (He's Better than our Phones)   28
Day 8: The Fruit of Attention, God's Way, is Peace   30

Solitude, Deprivation, And Our Phone:
God Wired Us For Solitude

Day 9: God Created Us to Need Aloneness   34
Day 10: God's Antidote to Frenzy and Stress   36
Day 11: The Three, Intertwined Ingredients of Solitude,
        Waiting, and Hope   38
Day 12: Praying in Solitude is Powerful (and Not Optional)   40

To Connect or Not to Connect:
Phones' False Promises and God's Truths

Day 13: God Made Us for Meaningful Connection (Code for Love)   44
Day 14: Phone-Based Connections Are a Knock-Off of Real Life
        Connections   46
Day 15: The Vital Difference Between Encouragement and "Affirmation"   48
Day 16: If I Don't Know Them, Must I Talk to Them?
        Connection with Strangers   50

God's Rest for a Tired, Burned-Out World:
Reclaiming It From Phone Frenzy

Day 17: How Phones Chase Out the Rest God Wants for Us   54
Day 18: Embracing Slowing Down and Rest's Gifts   56
Day 19: Rest Lets Us Be Human, Creatures Beloved by God   58
Day 20: Rest Connects Us to the Gift of Recreation   60

Is Contentment All Our Souls Crave?
God, Phones, and the Discontentment Trap

Day 21: Contentment is About Being Enough (in God)   64
Day 22: Being Content is Tied to Being Grateful   66
Day 23: Why Jealousy and Contentment Can't Co-Exist   68
Day 24: The Promise of the Quiet Life   70

Have We Lost Our Vision? Eyes Beyond Our Phone
Screen, for the Things of God

Day 25: The Problem of Passivity in the Faith Life   74
Day 26: An Imagination Is a Terrible Thing to Waste   76
Day 27: Planning and Stewardship Are Key Parts of a Vision-Fueled Life   78
Day 28: Partnering with God Around the Notion of Vision   80

A Way Forward:
Phone Use for the God-Minded

Day 29: The Critical Role of Self-Control – for Faith and Phone Use   84
Day 30: Balance (and the Trap of Legalism) in Phone Use   86

ENDNOTES

INTRODUCTION

I remember the day I realized that my phone was an enemy.... posing as a friend.

It was a particularly frenetic afternoon, my four kids home from school and clamoring with competing needs. Two were snacking and arguing, one needed homework help, and the fourth was looking for shoes before dance class. And me? I kept ducking out of the fray every five minutes to compulsively check my email, a task that was wholly unnecessary. My phone presented itself to me as a life raft, a way to get out, to divert my mind from the mounting pressure. Yet even as I swiped and clicked, I hated it. I could feel the irony – that I was trying to escape chaos by adding to chaos. But I couldn't seem to stop.

The fact is, while our phones are helpful and valuable tools, they also constitute a continual temptation. We use our phone more than we want to and can't seem to put it down. Our fingers itch for it, or our eyes stay glued too long to the screen. I have wrestled with these situations many times, and I bet you have too. We find it difficult to live out our values when our phones are nearby.

What is this truly about? That's the question I asked myself that chaotic afternoon, when discouragement over my poor phone habits over-whelmed me... And I've asked it many times since.

Yes, our phones deliver convenience, efficiency, and amusement, three things our culture highly values. And yes, engineers who design phones have built them to exploit human psychology, making them uncannily appealing and even addictive. But is that all of it?

What I've come to see is that our phones interfere with our wellbeing at the soul level, and this is what makes their hold so threatening. The more we use them, the more they influence our inner person in subtle ways. Our phones whisper half-truths or lies about who we are as humans, what we need, and God's relevance in our lives. In this, they become no longer just a tool but eventually a crutch... and ultimately an idol.

This short book is an invitation to examine the ways that phones are affecting our souls, and our relationship with God. It's not an indictment of phones. Phones are the central tool of our lives, and definitely here to stay; there's no reason to condemn them. In any case, the problems don't reside so much in the phones themselves, but in our hearts – in their weakness, waywardness, and proclivity to love God's gifts more than the giver.

He is a good God, and we don't find life or satisfaction apart from him. When we continue in poor habits and wrongly use our phones, we forego his blessing while simultaneously grieving his heart. It's a no-win situation.

Over the next thirty days, we will journey through seven areas where our souls often stray into dangerous territory as we use our phones. These are presence, attention, solitude, connection, rest, contentment, and vision. We'll look at how God intends for us to use these gifts, and how our phones interfere.

The good news is that nothing about the modern landscape alarms God; he is not surprised at the difficulty we have in managing our phones, nor at the trouble our poor practices have created for us. Instead he is compassionate and capable; he longs to draw us into the health and freedom he has for us. He is, after all, the God who "widens the path beneath (our) feet, so that (our) ankles do not give way" (2 Sam. 22:37).

May we learn to walk well and gratefully in his wide path, letting go of sin and poor habits that our phones have quietly cultivated within us. And may these thirty days usher in greater flourishing in our lives, as we seek and obey him.

———————

PRESENCE

Our phones and presence:
God is with us more than our phones

DAYS 1 — 4

DAY 1 : THE GIFT OF PLACE

"Then the Lord God formed a man from the dust of the ground and breathed into his nostrils the breath of life, and the man became a living being." Genesis 2:7

———————————

PRESENCE means existing... somewhere, on this earth. It's us in our surroundings, the place where our bodies are located.

We are embodied creatures – body, mind, and soul all dwelling together – and our presence encompasses all of these. It's so normal to us, it's forgettable. And this leaves us open to abusing presence, without even realizing that we are. This happens when we send our minds off to some other place and dwell— an act of exporting ourselves. Our bodies remain present, but our minds become absent to our surroundings.

On one hand exiting our place isn't innately bad, and in actual fact it's often necessary. Consider the example of academic work, where a student sits on his chair but is somewhere else in his mind, doing the figures. This is an everyday occurrence.

The problem is that exiting our present moment by withdrawing our attention from the current sphere can be overdone... and in today's world, it very often is. This is because our phones make it incredibly easy to transport ourselves away.

Our phones make us believe we can be present to two places at once – where we're physically located and in the world of the phone. But the fact is, we are embodied creatures, created by God to be both finite and limited. So we can't actually be in two places at once. The best we can do is toggle back and forth between our actual world and our screen-based world— sometimes so fast we fool ourselves into thinking we have multi-presence powers.

But only God is omnipresent. And when we "leave" our surroundings to "go into" our phone, what we're actually doing is giving up presence in the here-now world. This turns out to be a huge gift to lose – departing the God-given to enter the man-made.

The biblical concept of presence teaches us that we are created beings, not Creator. And our wise, all-knowing, sovereign God placed us on earth at this time, in this place. We are each here, by design, for this slice of mankind's history – "for such a time as this" (Esther 4:14).

The here-now moment that we're actually living is the only one we've got, and it's in this moment that we're seeing, hearing, feeling, knowing, and being with. We live and grow when we're present to God, ourselves, and others.

And we lose all that when we exit.

———————————

PRAY:
God, we accept with gladness our status as created beings, beloved creations springing from your hands. You knit us in our mothers' womb before our life began, and you hold us here too – in this moment and on this acre. Help us see and receive your gift of presence. Help us know you in it.
Amen

REFLECT:
We believe that we can "multi-task," when research demonstrates that we can really only flit from one task to another quickly (losing efficiency in the process). Similarly, we believe that we can "multi-place" by being both in our phone and present to our surroundings. Do you try to "multi-place" often?

DAY 2 – THE PRESENT IS WHERE GOD SEES US

"She gave this name to the Lord who spoke to her:
'You are the God who sees me.'" Genesis 16:13

PRESENCE is about more than simply being aware that the moment
and environment in which we've been placed is a gift. It's also about the
reality that God resides with us, in a real (though invisible) way, in that
space. When we are present in our physical space, we can become
present to God.

The Bible is full of examples of often-oblivious people like us being
brought into the awareness that God is literally present, interacting with
them in that moment. Jacob wrestling with the invisible figure; Saul
on the road to Damascus; Mary speaking with Gabriel. Or my favorite,
Hagar – approached by an angel during her flight of despair, who says,
"You are the God who sees me." It changes her, and the whole direction
of her life.

Can we believe that the Lord sees us right now in all our minutiae – with
bleary eyes and messy hair, in traffic, late to our key meeting? Or that
he sees us in our moments of great trial – our epic fight, job loss, cancer
diagnosis?

We often look to our phones because we want to be entertained, to see
things that delight our eyes or perk up a dull moment. Or we look to our
phones because we want to be relevant, for others to see us, to be part
of other people's thoughts.

But if God sees us, we don't need to be entertained, because he's
already got us in an epic tale of intrigue, battle, loss, and redemption:
our own journey with him. And if God sees us, we don't need to be
relevant, because we're already cherished by the one person who matters
most in all this huge universe. His death for us is irrefutable evidence of
his devotion.

As we dwell on the truth that every moment we breathe and every tear we shed is known and precious to him, we can know that we're beloved by him. He is Emmanuel, "God with us," literally and profoundly. Our incarnational God came to earth for face-to-face fellowship, just to demonstrate that he is not far off but with us, personally.

How would we use our phones differently if we lived in the reality of this fact – that he is seeing and adoring us at this moment?

We can relish the present because being with him in real time is life's greatest joy and privilege. So let's not allow our phone use get in the way.

————————

PRAY:
God, it's easy to be unaware that you are present in this moment, seeing us. Your invisibility throws us, and we forget, wander, and sin. Remind us again that we are never out of your vision and that, as you see us, you are loving us wholly and ushering us through a meaningful journey that leads toward you in glory. Amen

REFLECT:
In Reconnect: Spiritual Restoration from Digital Distraction, *Ed Cyzewksi asks, "How can we experience 'God with us' if we aren't even aware of ourselves in the present moment?"* [1] *. It's the right question to ask. Think about your awareness of yourself in general, and also the times you are most cognizant of God's nearness to you. How does your phone play into those situations?*

DAY 3 : GOD MAKES US FREE IN THE PRESENT

"It is for freedom that Christ has set us free. Stand firm and do not let yourselves be burdened by a yoke of slavery." Galatians 5:1

———————————

ONE of the hardest things about modern life is how often we feel trapped or stuck because of our circumstances or surroundings. We're often fretful, tethered, weighed down, even before we pick up our phones.

Now enter the phones. All day long, a barrage of inputs comes at us fast and furious – the headlines, texts, constant ding of notifications from the device in our hand that is both our seeming lifeline... and our jailer.

When people spend time away from their phones, they initially experience some distress or anxiety, but then something interesting happens. They start to feel liberated. "I feel so free!" is the refrain of many who participate in my phone challenges or the digital detoxes I run.

Why do they say that?

Because when they remove themselves from their phones, they no longer feel pushed around by its many demands. They regain the role of master of the tool; the tool no longer masters them.

Matthew tells us that Jesus' compassion on people was "because they were harassed and helpless" (Matt. 9:26). These words also apply to how our souls feel when we overuse our phones. We feel enslaved and powerless, trapped.

This is a sad state, especially so because Jesus died to bring us freedom – a freedom that reaches us *minute by minute*. It's here in the present moment, in this very time and space, that Jesus wants to liberate us. That means anything that's *stealing* our freedom in this moment must be confronted and brought into submission.[2] In today's world our phone is most often the culprit, so it's the thing that we must wrestle with, through God's strength.

The freedom of God is not theoretical; it's actual. And it's glorious. We grieve the heart of God and do violence to our own souls when we continue living stuck.

Since we have the privilege and can experience the joy of living in freedom, knowing the goodness of God in our present moment – why would we prefer enslavement?

PRAY:
God, we confess that we too often go to our phone as a form of escape, thinking it will make us feel more free. Forgive us for falling into this trap, and for seeking a source for our freedom outside of you. Thank you for the sweet freedom we have in Jesus, a freedom that is all we need. Keep us from using our phone for escapism.
Amen

REFLECT:
Do you use your phone to "free yourself" from a moment that feels too intense or boring? Conversely, do you also feel harassed and helpless around your phone sometimes – like you always need to check and respond, stuck in a loop? Think about what it means that you are free because of Jesus, and your phone need have no hold. If you have never tried a phone challenge or digital detox, consider implementing a short one.

DAY 4 : WE WALK WITH GOD IN THE PRESENT MOMENT

"In your presence is fullness of joy." Psalm 16:11

————————————

IN today's world, we tend to think of our phone as our one, true, vital companion. We can't leave home without it. It keeps us company, filling our hands, our minds – and our minutes. In the early years of the smart-phone's advent, Wendy Speake writes of a woman who "introduced" Speake to her phone, referring to it as her boyfriend. "Her husband laughed at the adulterous way she clung to it," she writes, "always splitting her time and attention between her two loves."

The phone-as-boyfriend concept illustrates the way we live with our phone, think about it, and share life with it intimately each day. Our present moment is very often dominated by it.

When we use our phone this way, as a primary source of companionship, we miss the beautiful reality of God's rightful place in our life. He wants to give us joy and abundant life in meaningful ways... and he does this by walking with us. It's as we communicate with him and turn our hearts toward him that we gain the riches of his goodness, joy, peace, comfort, and wisdom. He gives these to us continuously as we connect with Him in real time.

The monk Brother Lawrence, a humble cook in a French monastery in the 1600's, writes of this in his famous *The Practice of the Presence of God:* "There is no sweeter manner of living in the world than continuous communion with God."[4] Paul's words in Acts 17:28 capture the essence of this: "In him we live and move and have our being." God's invitation to be with him is ongoing and unchanging... and the present moment is the only one we have to respond.

But we cannot have a close intimate relationship with our phone *and* with God as we walk through our life. Our present moment can't accommodate our heart's allegiance to both. Either our heart and interest are turned toward our phones, or they're turned toward God. The first brings diversion, entertainment, even superficial happiness for a time. But the second brings life, hope... and everything good and fruitful that our souls ultimately need.

The question is, who is dominating your present? Has your phone come to take the role in your life that should belong to God?

———————

PRAY:
God, we love our phones. It's easy for the minutes of our day to revolve around them, to trade the richness of daily companionship with you for the shallow, superficial substitute our phones can offer. Forgive us for our sin. Remind us that you made us for your-self, and our hearts find rest in you alone.
Amen

REFLECT:
What does it mean to you that the only place we can connect with, worship, or be fulfilled by God is in the present moment? How often does your phone compete for that sacred space? Some experience the tension between phone and God for the pre-eminent role as an observable struggle, whereas for others it is nearly entirely subconscious. What about you? Brainstorm practical ways in which you can be more intentional about choosing God as your daily companion.

ATTENTION

What's so great about attention?
God wants it; phones steal it

DAYS 5 — 8

———

DAY 5 : ATTENTION: "NOT FOR SALE"?

"I keep my eyes always on the Lord. With him at my right hand, I shall not be shaken." Psalm 16:8

_____

ATTENTION means applying the mind to something, intentional listening or watching. We humans have a unique capability among created beings: to pay attention to *anything we want*, not just whatever's before us. This is a gift, and also something that can easily be turned into temptation or liability.

"Pay attention!" a teacher barks at a student who's supposed to be listening but isn't, and we cringe inwardly because we can so relate. Most people find it very easy to pay attention to things that *interest* them but hard (sometimes painfully) to pay attention to things that don't.

Attention is unique to people, a fascinating reality that permeates our humanness. We have a finite amount of it, like time or money – only so many minutes in a day or dollars in the bank. Once they're gone, they're gone... and we don't get them back. Attention is like this.

In today's economy, attention is a highly valuable commodity. Marketers use the term *"attention-harvesting,"* which means getting people's "eyeballs on the screen to sell attention to advertisers."[5] In this, our phone uses us as much as we use it. "Your phone works for a company in California, not for you," writes John Mark Comer in *The Ruthless Elimination of Hurry.* "You're not the customer; you're the product. And it's your attention that's for sale."[6]

Demands for our attention come at us constantly, distracting and breaking concentration. Our screens, especially our phones, amplify these interruptions. We're conditioned to the continual ding from our back pocket coming at us dozens of times a day. It's made us the most distractible people who've ever lived.

But healthy development of our minds and souls can't happen without sustained attention.

God wants us to live purposefully and pay attention to the things that truly matter; the Bible's full of instructions to focus on the important and eternal. This isn't because God wants to bore us but because he knows what's good for us. When our attention is on him, he's at our "right hand," as today's verse says, and therefore we "shall not be shaken."

This puts us in the middle of a battle. Our phones' ask us to focus on our ever- changing, handheld words and images. But God desires our attention to be on him and his kingdom. It takes *work* to prioritize and attend to God, but it's worth it – and he rewards us.

_____

PRAY:
God, you give us power to focus and choose what to focus on. Thank you for this gift. Make us mindful of those who would strip our attention away from things that matter (most of all, you), and give us wisdom and strength to resist them. Keep our phones from distracting us in unhealthy ways, and keep us from squandering our attention on worthless things.
Amen

REFLECT:
Think about your dog (or one you know) and the limits of its mind. It can't reflect on yesterday, read a book, or plan for tomorrow. We humans, conversely, can direct our mind to attend to anything we want. Estimate the percentage of the time you attend to things intentionally, versus the percentage your attention "goes where it wants." How does phone use play into these dynamics?

DAY 6 : ATTENTION: WHAT WE LOOK AT, LISTEN TO, AND ACTUALLY DO

"Let your eyes look straight ahead; fix your gaze directly before you. Give careful thought to the paths for your feet and be steadfast in all your ways." Proverbs 4:25-26

———————————

YOU give attention to what you view, listen to, and think about. You *look* at your friend's eyes when trying to give him focus. You *listen* to the lyrics of a new song you love. You *think about* what you're going to have for dinner (even at 11 AM, in the car). These are our primary attention portals –eyes, ears, and brain.

God's got something, or many things, to say about all of them. Here's one for seeing: *"Turn my eyes away from worthless things;"* (Ps. 119:37A). One for hearing (with Jesus as the speaker): *"Whoever has ears, let them hear."* (Matt. 11:15). One for thinking: *"With minds that are alert and fully sober, set your hope on the grace to be brought to you when Jesus Christ is revealed"* (1 Pet. 1:13).

We're supposed to have eyes, ears, and brain-space available for God and his ways – things related to truth, goodness, beauty. But we're saturated with the here-now of our world – with diversions, task lists, entertainment. We get maxxed out by duty and by pleasure; our phones fill up the remaining space on our internal hard drive.

So we don't see the things God's doing in our midst, hear his still, small voice, ponder his words or communicate with him in our hearts. We know those things are important, but we don't have focus for that.

Oh, we *want* to have attention for God and his ways, we mean and plan to – for sure. But not right now. We know it's honors him and benefits us. But so often we lack follow-through, and our best intentions don't pan out. So our attention goes to the most interesting thing of the moment – often found in our phone. And there it stays.

Attention and self-control are close cousins; it takes practice to harness attention and turn it to the things we wish to focus on. When we find a gap between what we *mean* to and what we *actually* attend to" – we can catch ourselves and ask God to help us grow in self-control to redirect attention to him. We can trust him to answer this prayer.

This is what "steadfast" in today's verse means – *"Give careful thought to the paths for your feet and be steadfast in all your ways."* Think about your way, the psalmist says, and then make your feet walk in it. Tie your attention to your actions. Make it happen and attend to God. It's worth it - and he rewards us.

———————————

PRAY:
God, we confess our lack of self-control and failure to follow through on good intentions. Forgive us for looking at, listening to, and thinking about many things more than about you. Guard our eyes and ears and thoughts, that they may be focused on you. Keep us from over-using our phones, and make us steadfast. Amen

REFLECT:
Consider a typical day and identify the things you most enjoy looking at, listening to, and thinking about. Where do you go when you have a spare minute, or when you're looking for a quick hit of comfort? These comprise the 'greatest hits' reel for your attention. Ask God if he would have you adjust your habits, in even small ways, to be "steadfast in all your ways" toward him. What phone adjustments might you make to support this effort?

DAY 7 : IN THE CONTEST OF ATTENTION, GOD WINS (HE'S BETTER THAN OUR PHONES)

"Because your love is better than life, my lips will glorify you." Psalm 63:3

_____

THE key thing to realize about attention and where to put it is: God is *actually* awesome. This may seem obvious but needs to be said because first, we don't fully believe it, and second, we don't remember it.

It takes work to believe that God is the best thing in our life; it doesn't always feel that way. When Jesus' followers asked what to do to please God, Jesus said, "The work of God is this: to believe in the one He has sent." (John 6:28-29) The believing itself is enormously difficult, sometimes requiring wrestling or even tears to hold onto faith.

Even when we *do* believe he's the best we've got, we often forget. Forgetfulness is one of our most human qualities. The Bible is full of God telling his people to remember his goodness and faithfulness – because they constantly don't. And we don't either.

If we don't believe or remember that God is good, we won't want to pay him much attention – if any. He won't seem worth it. But when we do believe and can remember – then paying him the attention he deserves is a lot more realistic. It's also self-reinforcing, because the more attention we pay him, the more we experience his goodness and then want to keep paying him attention. It becomes what psychologists calls a virtuous cycle.

Our phones keep us distracted, which always hurts us. If we doubt God, our phones buffer us from distilling that truth and wrestling with him over it (in the way he wants us to, as evidenced in at least half of the

Psalms). If we're unfocused, our phones further splinter our attention... and fill us with diversions and the 'tyranny of the urgent', to the point where God seems irrelevant and not worth remembering.

But God **is** better than anything in our phones, or any hope or goal we're trying to reach *through* our phones. He's better than anyone in our contact list. He's better than Pinterest – the house we go there to dream about. Better than Instagram – and the affirmation we look to gather there. Better than Tiktok –and the fun and amusement we seek. He's better than *all of it*.

When we believe and remember that God and his love are the very best – literally better than our lives – then we will have attention for him. We will have the *will* to attend to him... and to keep our phone and all its "lesser things" in their proper place.

PRAY:
God, we often don't believe that you're as good as you are, or that you're enough for us. Help us to say, with the man whose son was blind, "Lord I believe; help my unbelief." (Mark 9:23) Reveal your goodness to us, empower us to release our hold on things like our phones that distract us, and may we hold tight to you - the one thing that is truly worthy of our attention.
Amen

REFLECT:
When the psalmist says, "Your love is better than life," does that seem real... or idealistic? Consider your experience of God's goodness and love for you. Do you fall more into the "unbelief" or "forgetfulness" camp when it comes to God's love for you? Now think about ways that you can stay more mindful of his goodness in practical ways. Consider whether changing your phone lock-screen or playing worship music could change your phone habits from God-absent to God-focused.

DAY 8 : THE FRUIT OF ATTENTION, GOD'S WAY, IS PEACE

"You will keep in perfect peace those whose minds are steadfast, because they trust in you." Isaiah 26:3

THE point of paying less attention to your phone and its distraction isn't just to pay less attention to it. And the point of paying more attention to God and his ways isn't just to pay attention to God. Those are means to an end, not the end in and of itself.

So what is the end?
The point of attention, properly directed to our creator, is to be one with him. We are made to be united to Christ. Jesus told the father: "I have given them the glory that you gave me, that they may be one as we are one— I in them and you in me." (John 17:22)

When we are united to Christ, we share in his glory and joy... and also his peace. We get the benefit of being deeply bonded with the Prince of Peace in our inner places, realizing that his attention is forever on us.

The way we get to unity with Christ is a steadfast mind. This is Paul's message about "taking captive every thought to make it obedient to Christ." (2 Cor. 10:5). It's an intentional mental exercise to keep our thoughts laid out before Jesus' eyes, revealed and surrendered. We will never do it perfectly, this side of heaven, but God asks only for best effort, not perfection. He wants us to keep returning to him even when we mess up. This is "steadfastness."

I want peace, more than most things. I have four kids and find few things harder than the squabbles and conflicts among family members. When a kid picks at a sibling, or two start going at it, it crushes something inside of me. I feel I'd do anything to make.the.fighting.stop.

In situations like this, we follow shortcuts that we think will lead to peace. When we're stressed and need a mental 'out,' we often go to our phones. We check our email, our social media feeds, the news. We believe escaping that tension in a moment will provide release.

But the truth is, no one ever returns from escapism to their phones in a posture of peace and contentment. We come back more frazzled than we left... or else zoned out, glassy-eyed, disengaged. Neither of these reflect peace.

God is saying the solution to this panicked state of anxiety is a steadfast mind, with our attention continually returning to him in a posture of trust. He can give us what our screen-fueled world just never can: peace. Real, lasting, permeating peace.

PRAY:
Jesus, you are the Prince of Peace, stiller of every storm. There is no conflict that exists within us or between us and others that you can't still. Help us believe it's worthwhile to put our attention fully on you – that you will reward us as we do so. Help us to seek you and your peace that passes all understanding, not our phones. Amen

REFLECT:
John Eldredge created the Pause app because he felt it was important to have a place to go – on our phones – to catch our breath and center on Jesus and his peace.[7] Apps like Pause can be surprisingly effective ways to tap into the peace Jesus brings when in the midst of a busy day. If you haven't tried such apps, consider experimenting with one.

SOLITUDE

Solitude, deprivation, and our phone:
God wired us for solitude

DAYS 9 — 12

DAY 9 : GOD CREATED US TO NEED ALONENESS

"At daybreak, Jesus went out to a solitary place." Luke 4:42

AS humans, we *must* have time alone to flourish. You wouldn't necessarily know that today, because we prefer connection to being by ourselves. But social scientists are catching up to the reality that without solitude, we wither and falter. In *Digital Minimalism*, Cal Newport coined the term "solitude deprivation," which he defines as "a state in which you spend close to zero time alone with your own thoughts and free from input from other minds."[8] It leads to a host of negative outcomes.

This isn't new news. God built the need for solitude into our being. Even Jesus, the perfect man, needed solo time. When we're alone we have space and privacy to think our own thoughts, feel our own feelings, day-dream, and process hard things. It's where we get perspective and can see ourselves in relationship to a wide, complex world.

But we moderns generally hate to be alone – unless we have something to watch, scroll, photograph, video, post, or listen to. We've programmed ourselves to shun the quiet moment, and to fill any potentially solitary times with... our devices. Most often, our phones.

The two reasons we need to be alone are: first, we need to know ourselves, and second, we need to connect with God. These things both happen, and can only happen, in the quiet of our inner spaces. The Bible often references internal processing that happens in quiet spaces – "in the morning," (Ps 5:3) "on my bed" and "through the watches of the night" (Ps. 63:6). It assumes times of solo reflection where deep work can occur within our hearts and minds.

The self-reflection that comes when we're alone brings us to a place of reality, and this prompts internal shifts that can lead to maturity. Henri Nouwen says, "In solitude I get rid of my scaffolding (so it's) just me, ...

naked, vulnerable, weak..."[9] Vulnerability and weakness sound unappealing, so we avoid being alone.

But solitude, for the Christian, is a paradox as well as a doorway into transcendence. When we're alone, we discover we're actually *not* alone. Our limits bring us face to face with the limitless one. In the place of quiet we see ourselves as we are – and God as he is.

In solitude we experience his infinite love for us, the same love that led Jesus to die for us. And there we can detect his whispers, too quiet to be detected in the bustling marketplace of our daily lives. As Elijah discovered, "After the earthquake came a fire, but the Lord was not in the fire. And after the fire came a gentle whisper" (1 Kings 19:12).

So let's get alone, know ourselves... and hear him!

PRAY:
God, we admit that we like to distract ourselves more than we like to be alone. We confess we prefer diversions to seeing ourselves honestly, or to seeking you. Forgive us for our unwillingness to get alone. Help us put aside our phones and seek you in stillness. Amen

REFLECT:
How do you do with being alone without device, radio, or inputs of any kind? Does it make you feel bored or stressed? Try this experiment: set a timer for eight minutes (then move the device to the other side of the room!) Notice yourself, your thoughts, your emotions, your tendencies. What happens in your mind and heart?

DAY 10 : GOD'S ANTIDOTE TO FRENZY AND STRESS

"Then, because so many people were coming and going that they did not even have a chance to eat, he said to them, 'Come with me by yourselves to a quiet place...'" Mark 6:31

_____

STRESS has skyrocketed in our world by every marker – mental health challenges, addictions, suicide rates, you name it. Ours is an intense and harrying world: the to-do list long, the pressure on.

Often when people are harried, they reach for their phones – because they can divert us from what's causing distress. Phones have become a tool that we use to regulate our emotions, especially when we feel anxious or down. As sociologist Sherry Turkle says, it's not just that people want what their phones provide, it's also that they "don't want what their phones allow them to avoid... Going to your phone makes it easier to avoid... anxiety."[10]

Jesus offered people a different way. Because though daily stressors may have been lower in Bible times – no dings or buzzes, no road rage – lives were still bustling and taxing. There was no less *anxiety* then. Feeling harried, overwhelmed, and rushed have been around since creation. And Jesus spoke directly into it.

"Come with me by yourselves to a quiet place," he said in today's verse. He preached solitude, straight up – preached it and modeled it. He knew that the space of solitude would center and refresh, and he prioritized making that time. Today, to do as Jesus bids and "come away to a quiet place" involves a decision that's centered around our phone.

Will we bring our phone with us into the quiet place? This is the question.

Logistics require that we have it with us, or so we tell ourselves. But when our phone is in our hand, we can't fully "come away." Our brains simply behave differently when our phone is nearby, and our souls are affected. We can't enter the quiet, because our phones are never really silent.

Often, then, the choice to come away with God into solitude is a question of obedience. Obeying God would mean leaving the phone behind. Rationalizing our constant need for it and bringing it with us often signals our disobedience.

Ultimately, we must ask ourselves how serious we are about ditching stress, as God empowers, and living the abundant life that Jesus promised. We must ask how much we want to experience the refreshment that he's able to give. Because if we are serious, we will need solitude. And this means putting aside our phone.

PRAY:
God, we are anxious people, and though phone use increases anxiety... we still turn to it, again and again. We overuse our phone while under-utilizing your gift and provision of solitude. Thank you for the compassion you have for us in stress, and for making a way for us to experience your peace through solitude. May we embrace quiet moments, that we might know ourselves – and love you – better.
Amen

REFLECT:
What times of day (or in a week) do you generally feel most harried or overwhelmed? What do you typically do to combat stress in those moments, and do your strategies work- do they usher in a deep, penetrating peace? Experiment with swapping out times of solitude for phone use – choosing to take a few minutes of silence rather than defaulting to inputs like music or podcasts.

DAY 11 : THE THREE, INTERTWINED INGREDIENTS OF SOLITUDE, WAITING, AND HOPE

"For God alone, O my soul, wait in silence, for my hope is from him." Psalm 62:5

———————————

THROUGHOUT the Bible we see people waiting for God. God tells Abraham that he'll father many nations, but it's three decades till his wife finally conceives Isaac. There are thirteen years between Joseph's sale into slavery and his becoming viceroy over Egypt. The Israelites spend eighty years in captivity in Babylon... and later, they wait 400 years between the last words of prophecy and Jesus' birth. (And this is just a small sampling.) The word "wait" is used 150 times in the Bible. God does things slowly, requires patience, and expects his people to wait. He *does* answer prayer and fulfill his promises... but usually not quickly.

But we humans are impatient creatures; we're *born* impatient. From toddlerhood, we want things NOW! And when we don't get them, we grow distressed and distrustful. Deep within ourselves, we feel overlooked, abandoned, or wronged. We begin to despair.

God-directed waiting is an act of trust. In the quiet place we say, "I'm uncomfortable or hurting, but I'm going to believe you hear my prayers –and that you're good and have good for me." Waiting itself becomes a form of prayer; God-directed waiting is a central feature of biblical prayer, featured in dozens of Psalms. Together waiting and prayer paint a picture of hope, an expectation of positive things God will bring in the future.

Hope is so important to God and the life of the kingdom that it makes his top three core values – faith, hope, and love (1 Cor. 13:13). He is a God of hope.

It can be hard to remember this in our culture, which is obsessed with instant fulfillment. Quicker is always considered better – faster meals, delivery, downloads. We hate inconvenience, and therefore we hate waiting.

This is one reason phones have such a powerful hold on us. They fill waiting time and help us forget we *are* waiting. They feed self-absorption, responding to our internal voice saying, "Why should you have to waste your time like this? You're better than that."

They lie. Our phones do not have life, and therefore they cannot be a source of hope.

The psalmist commits to waiting in stillness and silence, because that's the space where his soul can meet with God. He knows his waiting will be fruitful because it will connect him with God. It's a waiting that brings hope, the one thing he needs to overcome his struggle.

We don't need our phones to flourish. We only need God to flourish. And to get to him, especially in the uncomfortable moment... we need to be willing to be alone, pray, and wait. This is how he brings us hope.

PRAY:
Father, thank you for doing important things in us as we wait, for shaping our souls in ways that grow us and please you. Forgive us our unwillingness to wait, and for trying to sidestep waiting times with our phones. May we experience and embrace the hope that comes from solitude and waiting.
Amen

REFLECT:
When in your life have you found it most difficult to wait for or hope in God, and how have you handled that challenge? Consider the relationship between waiting and hope – the ways are we tempted to find hope in our phones instead of the living hope that comes when we trust in God.

DAY 12 : PRAYING IN SOLITUDE IS POWERFUL (AND NOT OPTIONAL)

"But when you pray, go into your room, close the door and pray to your Father, who is unseen. Then your Father, who sees what is done in secret, will reward you." Matthew 6:6

A big challenge for us moderns in our tech-driven world is that our discomfort with being alone hampers our prayer life. When we're alone, we usually reach for our cell phones to do something "productive" or to drive away feelings of loneliness with (any type of) connection. This is such a kneejerk reaction that most of us don't even think about it.

When we habitually distract ourselves with our phones and screens, being alone feels increasingly awkward and uncomfortable. We can find it intolerable and so avoid solitude whenever possible. With this mindset, we can't possibly make prayer a priority.

But one of God's intentions for us in our times of aloneness is for us to pray. He wants us to create a closed-off space where we can engage in conversation with him in a regular way, just us and him. This is the Christian concept of the "prayer closet." It's a private place where the deep parts of us can connect with God.

This type of solo prayer is the opposite of the public communication we're so used to – no broadcast, livestream, running captions over our spoken words so viewers can read along. No viewers or listeners at all, in fact – just God.

You see, we have a God who sees what is done in secret. He created us and was there before the beginning of our lives – "when (we) were woven together in the depth of the earth, (his) eyes saw (our) unformed bodies." (Ps. 139:15-16) The secret place where we dwell, just with him, is a sacred and intimate space – and he prizes it. He invites us to prize it, too.

There are many rewards to a robust prayer life in the quiet place. As we pray, the Holy Spirit enters the process and intercedes for us (Rom. 8:26-27). We know God's nearness to us, and this fills us with hope. He helps us become more like Jesus. As we pray, we are filled with joy, peace, and perspective that fuel us.

But it starts with solitude – with turning off our phone, or putting it away. We follow that with the simple act of going into our room and shutting the door. Or getting into the car by ourselves, or going on a prayer walk. It's an intentional act. And it's a privilege.

————————

PRAY:
You call us to pray and tell us you see and reward what is done in secret. Thank you for your willingness to meet with us exactly as we are – no pretense, buffer, mediator, alternate audience. Just us and you. Thank you for the immense privilege of this kind of prayer. Empower us to meet regularly with you in this way, for our good and your glory.
Amen

REFLECT:
Does phone use reduce the amount of time (or interest) that you have for prayer? Do you spend time getting alone to pray? Think about the places in which you pray most fruitfully, and resolve to get into that space often, phone-free, in the coming days.

CONNECTION

To connect or not to connect:
phones' false promises and God's truths

DAYS 13 — 16

DAY 13 : GOD MADE US FOR MEANINGFUL CONNECTION (CODE FOR LOVE)

"A new command I give you: love one another. As I have loved you, so you must love one another." John 13:34

———————

THERE was a time when a telephone was used for one thing: talking voice to voice with another person. It's what it was invented for, and it's all it did. For over a hundred years the phone was only about connection: bringing people together for one-on-one talking and listening. The iPhone came out in 2007, and now phones are wholly different. They're sometimes about connection but often not. They can be a mirage of connection but an actual experience of disconnection.

Connection matters because it's the foundation for relationship. We were made for relationship by a relational God, and it's in relationship that love occurs. There we can be known and cherished – regardless of our flaws – and in return we can know and cherish others. And it starts with God, our creator, who knows us best and loved us first. He created us *because* of love, and because he wanted relationship with us.

The challenge is that not all connection leads to real relationship (or love), so not all connection satisfies. The soul wants *meaningful* relationship – wants to be both seen and valued. This kind of connection can be hard to find and takes time to cultivate. Often we end up settling for any old interaction or contact. Eventually we accept the counterfeit as the best we're going to get... but our souls never stop craving meaningful connection – and the love behind it.

Phones sometimes help with fruitful connection, like when we FaceTime friends or send encouraging messages. But often they hinder it, providing a setting that keeps relationships superficial. People text to avoid conversations. Social media users see events in a hundred friends' lives but know details (and hardships) of few. Influencers are followed by thousands but loved by none.

Fundamentally, the phone tells a lie about connection. It says, "the more you use me, the more connected you'll feel. I'll help you meet your soul's need for being known and loved." But the phone is not God and can't deliver on that promise. Research shows that phone users find that the more they use their device, the lonelier they feel.

God is not in a screen, and neither are your family members and friends. To love well we must connect meaningfully... and we can't do that well through a phone.

Let's love well, and let's not let our phones get in the way.

_____

PRAY:
Father, we don't want to believe lies... but we confess we have bought into the false promises of our phone. We acknowledge that it disconnects as much as it connects, and that when we over-use it, we love poorly. Forgive us. We would follow your command to love one another well, and we ask for your help. Amen

REFLECT:
When did you get your first phone? Whether you were 11 or 25... think about what your life was like, in terms of connection with others, before you got it. How is it different now, for better and worse? What are the primary differences between connections you engage in mainly online versus connections you engage in mainly in real life?

DAY 14 : PHONE-BASED CONNECTIONS: THE KNOCK-OFF OF REAL LIFE CONNECTIONS

"Above all, keep loving one another earnestly, since love covers over a multitude of sins. Show hospitality to one another." 1 Peter 4:8-9

––––––––––––––

RELATIONSHIPS in real life (IRL) are *hard*. People are flawed and selfish, and they hurt us – intentionally or unknowingly. In our relationships with others, we are guaranteed to sometimes feel disappointed, rejected, and wronged.

Since this is true, we are sometimes tempted to avoid others altogether. We know, however, that relationships are *also* the setting in which we experience the love our souls were built for; we can find it nowhere else. And God tells us to prioritize loving him and others well, above all things. While we live on this earth, loving well will be hard, he tells us – but also, beautiful, fruitful and entirely worth the effort.

But phones play tricks on relationships. They present a unique and constant temptation: to minimize in-person connections and maximize screen-based ones. As our phones' bells and whistles engage us, we may increasingly spend time interacting there... and eventually prize the people "in our phones" over off-screen people in our lives. Think of the friend who keeps ducking out of conversation to text or check social media. The mom who habitually ignores her child in favor of her phone.

There's a reason folks prefer their phones. Connections there feel more interesting than in-person relationships, and they're certainly easier to manage. They give us the illusion of being in community but ask nothing of us. We don't need to "show hospitality" to the influencers we follow on social media or "earnestly love" the faceless PTO mom on our text thread. We don't need to do anything more or less than tap keys or click buttons.

But here's the truth: one well-tended relationship is worth a thousand social media connections. As the Proverbs say, "A man of many companions may come to ruin, but there is a friend who sticks closer than a brother." (Prov. 18:24). The masses on social media are the counterfeits to connections that enrich our lives; the brother-like friend is the real thing.

When we prioritize screen-based connections over our IRL people, we subtly complain to God about the relationships he's provided for us. It grieves him when we prefer a sea of surface connections to the real relationships God has given us, customized gifts he wants us to nurture and cultivate.

———————————

PRAY:
Lord, we are too often lazy, preferring easy connections in our phones that ask nothing of us over our in-person relationships that are sometimes hard. Forgive us for seeking the connection 'quick fix' in our phones. Banish our selfishness and make us mature and whole – in Christ's name, and for his glory.
Amen

REFLECT:
We often apply different standards to people we observe versus ourselves, including when it comes to phone use. Think of a time when you were unable to get someone's attention because they were fixated on their phone… and a time when you clearly ignored someone in order to tend to tasks on your phone. Consider how each one made you feel.

DAY 15 : THE VITAL DIFFERENCE BETWEEN
ENCOURAGEMENT AND "AFFIRMATION"

"Therefore encourage one another and build one another up, just as you are doing." 1 Thessalonians 5:11

———————————

IN our era, often the first thing a person does when she's having a low moment is pick up her phone. We look to phones to tell us whether we're "doing OK" in the world – to assess whether people care about us or like us. Social media is the main culprit.

We ride and fall on the approval of others. Teens who feature in the documentary "Liked," admit that they take down a social media post if it garners fewer than 100 likes.[11] Too few affirmers make them feel that the post – and they themselves – are unacceptable.

In *12 Ways Your Phone is Changing You*, Tony Reinke says, "Many of us are addicted to our phones because we crave immediate approval and affirmation."[12] And phones do condition us to seek and relish the praise of man. Reinke says, "Phones prick the primitive human impulse for appreciation... through constant contact with other seekers of affirmation."[13] We're the needy, seeking the needy, hoping for gains in self-esteem.

There are two main problems with this. The first is that our creator and redeemer tells us to live for him and his approval alone. Jesus modeled for us a life lived solely for his father: "I try to please the one who sent me" (John 5:30). Seeking affirmation from others upends this, as we can't serve two masters (Luke 16:13).

The second is that social media style affirmation is a cheap imitation of encouragement, not the genuine good that our souls need. Encouragement means to make someone "more determined, hopeful, or confident" (Merriam-Webster); it's providing sentiments of worth grounded in truth and context.[14] The primary encourager is God himself in the form of the Holy Spirit – the "encourager" and "spirit of truth" (John 14:16-17).

You see, encouragement and truth go hand in hand. It isn't an ego stroke; it doesn't compliment your outfit or insert a heart emoji. Instead the one who encourages gives support in a whole-person spirit, in a relational context that makes the encouragement trustworthy.

When we encourage someone we truly build him him up, reminding him that he's enough as he is (regardless of flaws. This is because Jesus is enough, and he makes us all enough. This is because Jesus is enough, and he makes us enough. We don't need to grasp straws or take great selfies, fishing for favor. In him, we have all we need.

So let's encourage others aright, not with social media likes and comments but seeing the whole person, speaking life and truth. And for ourselves, let's seek encouragement from God and those who know us well rather than seeking empty affirmation through our phones.

———————————

PRAY:
Lord, make us like Jesus – living for an audience of one, serving one master, not currying favor among those whose approval doesn't ultimately matter. Thank you for the Holy Spirit our encourager, and Jesus whose death for us makes us wholly acceptable in your sight. We are enough, as we are, because of him. Amen

REFLECT:
Think of someone who's a true encourager in a meaningful way – who sees virtue or growth and calls it out, expressing it in a context that brings big-picture hope. What does it feel like when this person encourages you? Consider yourself: what kind of encouragement or affirmation do you generally give others?

DAY 16 : IF I DON'T KNOW THEM, DO I HAVE TO TALK TO THEM? CONNECTION WITH STRANGERS

"'Love the Lord your God with all your heart and with all your soul and with all your strength and with all your mind'; and, 'Love your neighbor as yourself.'" Luke 10:27

———————————

THESE words are the response when an expert of the law asks Jesus what he must do to inherit eternal life. The then asks Jesus what exactly is meant by "neighbor," and Jesus tells the famous parable of the good Samaritan. The good neighbor is the one who doesn't ignore the needs of his enemy but generously helps him in his distress.

Us? We'd settle for a neighbor who's simply aware of our presence next to them in line at a store and smiles or makes eye contact. Gold star if they say a friendly word.

Few people interact personably with their neighbor because their eyes are on their phones. Virtually everyone is looking at his or her phone. I know, because I'm often the worst culprit.

In *How to Break Up with Your Phone*, Catherine Price talks about the value of fleeting relationships – "brief interactions, often with strangers, that create a sense of connection. For example: a pleasant exchange with a waiter, a group cheer at a sports bar, or one of those oddly personal chats that seem to occur between strangers on a plane."[15] Such interactions, she says, have a "surprisingly dramatic effect on how connected we feel to society at large."[16]

Research confirms what God's been saying since creation: reaching out to others, whoever they are, causes our hearts to flourish. Those who give, receive.

The first step to loving our neighbor is *seeing* our neighbor. We can't love what we're too distracted and phone-consumed to see.

Humans today are desperate for environments of connectedness, people engaging one another in real-world ways. They'd love to exchange jokes with their grocery clerk or have their kid complimented by a sidewalk-passer. Who wouldn't prefer a world like that? (It would send the rising loneliness rates and skyrocketing mental health issues plummeting.)

We Jesus-followers can start by taking him at face value when he says, "Love your neighbor." He wants to reach the people of this earth through us. He wants to love *through us*. Will we let him?

As Wendy Speake says, "Opening my phone closes me off to others, but closing my phone opens me up to those around me."[17] Let's be people who are open, in all the best ways, to loving those we meet – everyone God puts in our path.

––––––––––––––––––

PRAY:
Author and sustainer of connection; you set your Word in the world. You speak, and we come alive. You give us power to speak life too. Forgive us that we take this privilege so lightly or ignore it altogether. Give us a will to put down our phones, eyes to see the people you'd have us speak to, and a heart to love them as you do.
Amen

REFLECT:
Think of a time when someone you didn't know was especially kind or attentive to you in a pleasantly surprising way. Now think about your typical demeanor when you are out "in the world" doing life. How attentive are you to others around you, what factors contribute to this, and what role does your phone play?

REST

Rest for a tired, burned-out world: reclaiming it from phone frenzy

DAYS 17 — 20

DAY 17 : HOW PHONES CHASE OUT THE REST
GOD WANTS FOR US

"This is what the Sovereign Lord, the Holy One of Israel, says: 'In repentance and rest is your salvation, in quietness and trust is your strength.'" Isaiah 30:15

―――――――――

WHEN we hear the word "rest," we're likely to picture a person slumped exhaustedly on the couch, feet on the coffee table... possibly binging on Netflix. And that *is* rest, in one form. Navigating this world is taxing and drains us, and rest means taking a break.

But it also means much more than that.

Rest, as God created and commands, is about releasing our grip on the world and remembering that we aren't God. Choosing to rest is an act of surrender, a laying down of the temptation to work, to *just do something*. It's denying ourselves and our frenetic impulses so we might experience the sufficiency of God. In rest we trust God and take in his goodness.

Screens (and especially our phones) work against this, almost as if they were waging a war. They are rest's enemy – ushering in an illusion of rest, without its benefits.

For one thing, screens stimulate us physically which is why experts recommend not using them for at least an hour before bed. They dysregulate sleep and add to fatigue. For another, engaging with devices keep us mentally "on," scanning data or listening for the ding. Our bodies and minds both can't relax properly when devices are nearby.

Most importantly, though, the inner rest we need almost never comes through devices because screens can't invigorate our souls. We don't emerge from scrolling and swiping – from our text threads and social media sessions – centered and recharged. And how do we feel after a four-hour Netflix binge? Groggy and spaced out.

God wants to genuinely refresh us. When he commanded Sabbath, his point was for us to stop working – for our *good*, and our souls' flourishing. Screen-based rest is an imposter.

Let's recognize that phones impede the kind of rest God made us for (and the kind that glorifies him). May we be willing to enter digital sabbaths – for an hour, a day, or longer – so we can be present to the one who calls us to rest, who actually refreshes us.

Our strength comes from trusting God, and the quietness he brings as we look to him.

PRAY:
Creator God, you designed our bodies, minds, and souls – and you know how we all need rest. Thank you for making provision for the rest we need, and for teaching us how to take it. As we follow you into fruitful ways of rest, refresh us by sharing yourself and your strength. May we discipline ourselves to lay down our devices and let you be God, trusting that you have good for us in that.
Amen

REFLECT:
How easy is it for you to rest? What do you do when you're tired? There's nothing wrong with watching a show to unwind, or checking social media when you're on a break. But if these are the only strategies you use for rest, you probably have a rest deficit. In what ways do your body, mind, and soul unwind best? Think about how you might prioritize these.

DAY 18 : EMBRACING SLOWING DOWN AND REST'S GIFTS

"Come to me, all you who are weary and burdened, and I will give you rest. Take my yoke upon you and learn from me, for I am gentle and humble in heart, and you will find rest for your souls. For my yoke is easy and my burden is light." Matthew 11:28-30

WE live our lives in a rush – always packing in more, always fighting lateness to the next activity. We're frenzied, hurried, harried. From curbside pick-up to microwaves to on-demand movies, everything helps us go faster... and adds to the Fast Is Best mindset.

This lifestyle is exhausting, and we all feel it. Our burdens seem heavy and we feel frazzled or like failures, unable to keep up. One thing exacerbates that sense of go-go-go, more than any other in the modern world. It's our phone.

We check our phones compulsively, ensuring we're "connected," double checking we're not missing anything. We keep an ear out for its ding and jump like Pavlov's dog when it comes. Our task-list apps drive us; our timer sounds when we're late. We enslave ourselves to our phones, rushing to do their bidding.

This is not the life, or the freedom, that Jesus died to give us. Because our souls crave rest.

We have a savior who not only knows how exhausting life is but actually reverses our weariness and takes our burdens from us. He longs to do this for us, invites us daily! He gives rest not just to our bodies, but also to our souls. The question is: do we want this kind of rest? Do we want quiet without dinging, fingers that don't itch, restorative sleep?

The cost is obedience to him, and trust in him that his rest is good. His rest is slow hours away from the bustle of the world, eyes open to him. Often this takes place outside, in God's natural playground, where our souls can find refreshment in his beauty. He meets us there, where "the heavens proclaim the glory of God" (Ps. 19:1), and he calms our frantic hearts.

The ironic truth is that it's actually *wise* to ignore the demands our clamoring phones bring us. We have the power to ignore them – can choose whether we want restorative rest from the carrier of our burdens, or fretful quasi-rest delivered by our screens. God lets us choose.

Let's put down our phones, slow down, and invest in real rest. God will honor our obedience, and our souls will thank us for the energy and perspective his type of rest will bring.

Our strength comes from trusting God, and the quietness he brings as we look to him.

────────────

PRAY:
God, we confess that productivity is an idol. We love to be busy and active, to rush and feel accomplished. Forgive us for loving it better than we love you, and for rejecting your gifts of slowing down. We are weary and burdened; please give us the rest you promise. And help us lay down our devices so we can enter it. Amen

REFLECT:
Think about your life and the speed at which you live it – is it slow, medium, fast, or insane? Consider how you feel about your speed, and try to identify someone whose speed (and sense of rest in life) inspires you. Do you believe God has the power, and the interest, to slow you down and bring fruitful rest into your life?

DAY 19 : REST LETS US BE HUMANS, CREATURES BELOVED BY GOD

"He will rejoice over you with gladness; he will quiet you with his love." Zephaniah 3:17

———————————

THE thing our phones most threaten to chase away is our humanness.

What does it mean that we are human creatures carefully crafted by a God who adores us? He made us limited beings, bound by time and space– we cannot be in two places at once or give half our brains to one thing and half to another. And we are embodied, so that the experiences that happen in our body matter. They affect our thoughts and our feelings. We are not floating brains (or hearts) in a jar.

But today's devices, and especially our phones, try to lure us into becoming machines. They have us clicking and swiping and pressing as if we were robots or cogs on an assembly line. Phones engage our *bodies* very little – we transport into a portal while our bodies sit passively.

Trouble is, we come most alive when we dwell fully on this earth – body, mind, and spirit. And when we neglect the gifts of our humanity, we suffer. God made the taste of newly baked bread to comfort and delight. He made the pop of a crackling fire to center and cheer. He made the sweet smell of spring growth as relief and promise after winter. The pleasures God gives us to delight our senses can't be replicated on a screen.

To be human, we must live well in the world. And rest is what allows us to become present to the tangible gifts around us that God wants us to relish. Rest carves out a space for us to simply be creatures. Excessive use of screens disembodies us, elevates what is machine-like in us, and erodes our humanity.

The most important thing about being human is that God made us, and loves us, as human beings. He honors humanity so much that he became human himself, taking on flesh to join us as embodied people – body, heart, and mind. We can use our phones less, avoid using it so much it *de*-humanizes us, and in this, we can know God better and flourish.

Let's lay down our phones and rest well, humans that we are, in his loving embrace. Let's allow him to quiet us, in all the ways, with his love.

———————————

PRAY:
God, we know that watching a video of the ocean is nothing like sitting next to the real one, and no recording of a song through our phone speaker will ever mimic listening to a master pianist play. Thank you for gifts of goodness and beauty, and the rest that helps us behold them. Forgive us for being lured by our phone's charms and ignoring your good rest. May we receive all you have for us, in our humanity.
Amen

REFLECT:
Think about the experiences in your life that make you feel the most human. Hot chocolate on a snowy day? Lingering at dusk to watch the sunset? Make your own short list. Consider how these relate to the concept of rest, for you. Now think about your phone. What features in your phone make you feel the most human, and which ones make you feel the most automated or machine-like?

DAY 20 : REST CONNECTS US TO THE GIFTS OF RECREATION

"God has filled (Bezalel) with... knowledge and all kinds of skills to make artistic designs... and to engage in all kinds of artistic crafts." Exodus 35: 31-33

REST is tied to refreshment, and even delight. Work means labor and task accomplishment, but when we rest, our psyche opens up and we can take in pleasure. We have time to notice and experience the things that bring joy, and the combination of not working and engaging with pleasant things replenishes us.

Oddly enough, rest that's actually restful – to mind, soul, and body – is often somewhat active. It might be tending a garden, doing a craft, cooking and eating a delicious meal, strolling a farmer's market. It's often what Cal Newport refers to in *Digital Minimalism* as "high-quality leisure" rather than "low-quality digital distractions."[18] Using our hands is an avenue to true recharging.

This is where we remember that God made us in specific ways with skills and interests that produce beauty... and that when we engage in those things, it brings us joy. When God gave Bezalel skills in craftsmanship, he did it not only so that Israel could obtain well-made, beautiful products but because Bezalel's engagement in craft enhanced Bezalel (and those around him). Doing things we are skilled at feels rewarding.

Parents see this as their children grow. One child has fun dribbling outside and shooting hoops. Another pulls out baking tools and tries a new recipe. A musically inclined kid strums his guitar, and an artistically-inclined one sketches. They're engaged and content with their tasks, and the byproducts are positive. The activities are varied, but each has the capacity to bring delight. Such activities, Newport's "high-quality leisure" are what we understand as God's gift of recreation, in its best and truest sense. It's soul-engaging and world-enlarging.

When we interact with our phone, and when we consume media (on any device), we substitute digital distraction for true recreation – at significant loss to our happiness and our souls' health.

Let's use our free time to rest in ways that honor God's gifts to us. It brings joy to both him and us, and it recharges our whole person in ways that screens never can.

PRAY:
Lord, it's so much easier to grab our phone when we have quiet minutes than to engage in hobbies. We feel too tired (and too lazy) for high-quality leisure. But you've made us for more than consumption and superficial amusement, and these don't replenish us in the deep places. Thank you for nurturing and nourishing us... through recreation. May we engage with joy.
Amen

REFLECT:
Try putting your experiences of rest in three categories. In the first, put inactive forms of rest: sleep or napping. In the second, put passive activities that rest your body like watching a movie or reading a book. In the third, put activities of leisure like baking, gardening, crafting, or practicing a sport. Which type of rest is easiest for you to engage in, and which is hardest? Why?

CONTENTMENT

Is contentment all our souls crave?
Phones and the discontentment trap

DAYS 21 — 24

———

DAY 21 : CONTENTMENT IS ABOUT BEING ENOUGH (IN GOD)

"The Lord is my shepherd, I lack nothing." Psalm 23:1

———————————

CONTENTMENT refers to a state of happiness or satisfaction; it means being at ease in our situation and in our mind. Contentment isn't easy to come by; today it feels harder than ever.

For one thing, living in a culture of plenty accustoms us to having much. We expect to always be able to choose and acquire, and it fosters greed and a kind of entitlement. We become a people who want, habitually, and spend time wishing for more.

For another, the more rattled we feel, the more discontent we become – and high phone use increases our sense of being rattled. We feel pushed and pulled by its demands and temptations, and our anxiety spikes.

Neither entitlement nor anxiety can coexist with contentment.

When God created humans, we were wholly fulfilled in our relationship with him as we dwelt with others on his good earth. When sin entered the world, though, all that changed. Suddenly God was no longer enough for us, and neither were his gifts. Discontentment became our default.

 But we *can* still find our contentment in God, and find soul satisfaction in him, saying with the psalmist, "The Lord is my shepherd, I lack nothing" (Ps. 23:1). We can let him fill us, training ourselves to look to him as our everything. This is his greatest desire for us – to fulfill us, as he alone has the power to meet our every need. God being our center *is* the abundant life that Jesus died to give us, and it's a picture of real contentment.

Looking to God more means using our phones less. They're engineered to cultivate a restlessness in us through flashes, eye-catching icons and buzzing. But when we go to our phones looking for contentment through novelty or distraction, we lose. We find the opposite; they make us less happy, not more.

The truth is, we become content by embracing humility... and obedience. Jesus commands us not to let our hearts "be troubled" (John 14:1), and he shows us the path to getting there. It's by resting in his father's embrace, and doing his will on this earth.

Will we put down our phones and take these calls seriously? Our contentment is riding on it.

PRAY:
Jesus, your life was a perfect model of contentment. You did your father's work (John 6:38), found peace and joy in it- regardless of the suffering it caused. Forgive us for believing that we know a better way to find contentment ourselves. We repent of our greed, entitlement, and anxiety. Grant us the contentment that only you can.
Amen

REFLECT:
Think of a time in your life when you were most content; what circumstances were at play in that season? What was it like for you from a spiritual standpoint, and what was your phone use like?

DAY 22 : BEING CONTENT IS TIED TO BEING GRATEFUL

"But if we have food and clothing, we will be content with that." Timothy 6:8

———————————

CONTENTMENT is tied to gratitude. Much research has been done on gratitude, and the findings are in: an appreciative demeanor makes people happier. The old adage about "counting your blessings" really does work. Gratitude enables people to "feel more positive emotions, relish good experiences, improve their health, deal with adversity, and build strong relationships."[19]

This aligns perfectly with what God tells us throughout the Bible – that life is found in acknowledging his goodness to us in all its forms. When we give thanks to God it's soul-opening; it honors him and enriches us at the same time.

But our phones present a significant challenge to giving thanks, or even wanting to. The tiny computer in our hand is like a small world over which we feel owner and master. We decide what color, which homescreen and lockscreen, what apps, which sounds, who to contact or follow, what to post. We are the orchestrator of our own small world, and the more we use our phone, the more we grow in this illusory sense of all-powerfulness. We experience ourselves as almost god-like.

Left unchecked, our phones make us largely self-consumed. And people who are self-consumed have a hard time being grateful. They don't even see the blessings in their lives – or if they do, they believe *they* are the ones responsible for them. Oblivious of the giver, they cannot even see the gifts. (And *every* good gift – our food, our clothes, the air we breathe – is from God.[20]) Over time, this hardens our hearts and warps our perspective. We become like bratty children, talking back to a generous parent.

The solution is to keep our phone in its place, literally and figuratively. We cannot afford to live in a world with our phone at the center. It untethers us from reality and falsely puts us at the center of our own world. Any gratitude that we can muster from this space will be shallow and inauthentic. It will be a head nod to God, with no power to connect us to him or transform us.

Let's remember that God graciously makes our phones available to us, one gift among millions. He didn't have to put us in a world where such ingenuity could flourish, or where such tools existed. Let's not abuse the gift, commandeer it, or confuse the gift with God himself. There is no lasting contentment down that path.

_____

PRAY:
God, we confess that we are prone to see ourselves as the center of the universe. You alone are God, and every good thing comes from your hand (James 1:17). Forgive us for blindness to your generosity, and for inserting ourselves in your place. Give us eyes to see our phones' role in perpetuating lies in our minds. May we please you.
Amen

REFLECT:
Think about how you feel when you use your phone frequently. Does it make you feel all-powerful? Do you feel invincible when it is in your hand, that you can "control the world" (or at least your own world) at the push of a few buttons? How might your phone use work against meaningful gratitude, or contentment, in your life?

DAY 23 : WHY JEALOUSY AND CONTENTMENT CAN'T COEXIST

"You desire but do not have, so you kill. You envy but you cannot get what you want, so you quarrel and fight." James 2:3

HOW much of your day is spent comparing yourself to others, pining for someone else's (fill in the blank), feeling that you lack something, or battling inadequacy? For many of us, it's more time than we care to admit. This is envy – the earth-old trait of wishing for things belonging to others. So common a feature is jealousy in the human heart that it has its own commandment among the ten.[21]

There are two key things to understand about jealousy: first, it's a vice. Second, it makes us feel terrible. (Scientists say it actually hurts to feel jealous, because sensors of envy and physical pain reside in the same zone of the brain.[22]) Nobody would knowingly choose to experience more of it in their lives.

And yet we set ourselves up for high levels of jealousy every day, by our use of social media. It's a breeding ground for envy. Social media is the place where we see posts of greatest hits of others' lives... and we watch them, sometimes in infinite doses. There is nothing wrong with posting good things in our lives (and it can even be an act of gratitude, recognizing blessings). But the effect of this practice in community, at scale, is usually envy and insecurity, because the shininess of others' lives makes our own life appear pale by comparison. The apps' designs take it further, intentionally inflaming jealousy through the use of likes and follower counts.

Once jealousy takes hold, it blocks even the possibility of being content. We can't be satisfied with what we have while gazing longingly at someone else's things (or life), seeing it as better and wishing it were our own. It's a wedge keeping us from God's loving heart.

The good news is that we don't have to be a victim of envy. When we find ourselves feeling jealous, we can choose to get out from under it. First, we can take note of what sparks envy and limit it - unfollow that person, reduce screen time, or get off social media altogether. Second (and more importantly), we can repent of our jealousy and ask God to rid our hearts of it. We can follow his path into gratitude and contentment.

Envy "rots the bones," (Prov. 14:30), but God's ways are good and rescue us from our worldly longing. Let's dwell there, and bask in the contentment only he can bring.

———————————

PRAY:
God, rid us of all envy, and help us live with the reality that when we have you, we have everything good - and all we need. Remind us of our true identity and the best gift of our life: that we are adored by our maker. May we release interest in blessings you have not given us, and become more grateful for the ones you have.
Amen

REFLECT:
In what areas of life do you struggle most with envy? Do you find that exposure to social media impacts your feelings about yourself or your life? Think about what steps or actions you have taken when you've felt jealous online that have helped relieve those feelings.

DAY 24 : THE PROMISE OF THE QUIET LIFE

*Make it your ambition to lead a quiet life: you should
mind your own business and work with your hands"
1 Thessalonians 4:11*

AS a society, we've developed a phone-driven norm of engaging with
The World Out There. We capture aspects of ourselves – a photo or
video, a talk or dance – and we export it for public viewing. We frame,
then share. Social media has made this not just possible but completely
expected. And there's nothing innately wrong with it.

The difficulty is that these actions have unintended consequences. As
we've seen, they work against gratitude, encourage comparison, and
breed envy. They also distract us from more important things, like living
well in the here-now life that God has given us.

When we focus on "out there" – whether consuming and reviewing
the finer points of other people's lives, or working to get our stuff out
into the world– we have less attention for our "right here" life. We get
distracted and our priorities go wonky.

Worse, our hearts get consumed with the marketplace of the masses,
buying and trading (so to speak) in their images, presentations, and
efforts toward relevance. We give our hearts and souls away to these
exchanges.

We are to have one true love, and it is to be God. Our life with him is to
be a personal, intimate, focused, two-person dance. This is hard to enact,
but it's the call and commitment of the follower of Jesus. We are to
minimize or even lay down distractions and competing demands on our
passion and time; nothing should get in the way of loving him.

This is the essence of the "quiet life" that Paul refers to in his words to the Thessalonians. Christians are to be steady, diligent, focused people, people not always looking at the world or at what the Joneses are doing. Paul encourages fruitful productivity in simple ways, almost a kind of minimalism. We are to live within our real-life spheres, busy with the tasks God has given us and stewarding them well.

Let's recommit to simplicity, letting God be enough for us, and being diligent in our God-given work. (And I think we can bet that swiping and scrolling on phones would not qualify as 'working with your hands'!)

———————————

PRAY:
God, we often want to busy ourselves with the "out there" world more than cultivate our "right here" opportunities – or tend our own souls in ways that please you. Forgive us for this. Help us to keep you as our first love and attend with joy the tasks you put before us, even difficult ones. We want to be diligent and obey you well. Help us, in the power of the Holy Spirit.
Amen

REFLECT:
What do you think of when you hear the directive to "lead a quiet life"? Does it sound boring, or appealing? What examples can you think of, biblical or real life, that display compelling or exciting things that happened for people when they were striving to faithfully "lead a quiet life" that was committed to the Lord?

VISION

Have we lost our vision?
Eyes beyond our phone screen, for the things of God

DAY 25 : THE PROBLEM OF PASSIVITY
IN THE FAITH LIFE

"Prepare your work outside; get everything ready for
yourself in the field, and after that build your house."
Proverbs 24:27

———————————

GOD wants us to be diligent people and lead active lives, doing good work that spreads his light and fulfills his purposes. The Bible is full of directives about this, with dozens appearing in the Proverbs. There are many against sloth, and more about planning and stewarding time and opportunity. God did not create us to just sit around. He's taking us somewhere... for something. We're on a journey.

A key ingredient in a rightly proactive life is vision: "thinking about or planning the future with imagination or wisdom."[23] It's forecasting with hopefulness. I love the Bible's picture of vision in Proverbs 31:16, the noble woman who "considers a field and buys it; out of her earnings she plants a vineyard." She takes planned steps to bring her vineyard idea from concept to reality.

Today, one huge obstacle to enacting vision in our lives is our phones.

That's because vision is proactive, goal-setting in nature – by definition it looks ahead and moves toward an identified *something*. But our phone does the opposite of look ahead. It keeps us wholly focused on the now: this text thread, that social media scroll, the "up next" YouTube clip already populating. It can keep us rooted on our couch for hours.

Phones cast a spell that robs us of our motivation and slowly bleeds our drive for (or even thoughts about) vision. They are portals of passivity.

They also make everything in our life so fast and easy ("there's an app for that!"), that over time our use of them erodes our planning muscles. Think about how outlandish it feels to use a paper map or written directions instead of GPS! Our phone-crutch gradually accumulates an internal laziness within us that works against proactive thinking.

But the fact is, God gave us the capacity for vision and goal-setting, and we need them to please him and lead faithful lives. If we are to fulfill God's purposes for our lives, we need clear eyes to see the road he's put us on, and ready wills to walk toward the destination.

Let's ditch the phone-spell and rustle up some God-directed proactivity!

―――――――――――

PRAY:
Lord Christ, we confess that we can be lazy and unmotivated. We'd rather sit and be entertained than get up and do the work that would enhance our lives or fulfill your kingdom purposes. We choose self and ease over others and tasks that feel arduous, and this grieves you. Help us follow your way, the way of self-denial, remembering that those who work are rewarded, and those who give receive.
Amen

REFLECT:
Think about times you have gone to your phone thinking you'd just spend a minute... and inadvertently screen-stared for an hour. How frequent an occurrence is this for you? Consider if your phone often tempts you to passivity or laziness. If so, what circumstances or apps foster this?

DAY 26 : AN IMAGINATION IS A TERRIBLE THING TO WASTE

"But blessed are your eyes because they see, and your ears because they hear." Matthew 13:16

IF you hear the term "imagination," it's probably related to children. That's about the only setting in which we talk much about imagination. But the gift of imagining isn't just something God intended for kids; it's for all of us.

The point of imagination is that it allows us to conceptualize things not immediately present. It's using our *mind's* eye instead of our physical eyes. This is part of vision. Oswald Chambers called imagination "the greatest gift God has given us," saying "it ought to be devoted entirely to him,"[24] and he's completely right.

Imagination empowers us to behold things that are not, a key first step in bringing an inkling to life. Through imagining, God lets us to see beyond the here and now and hear whispers still inaudible to others. It's the precursor to beauty, fuel for brainstorming, fodder for workable solutions, and main ingredient in inventiveness.

The reality is that God wants us to use our imagining faculties. He made us in his image and endowed us with the same type of creative capacity that he has. What an honor!

The problem is that many of us squander our imaginations. We don't do it consciously; we just fail to value them, and so they wither and fade to extinction from lack of use. We're simply too busy, and too distracted, to imagine new things.

Instead, we consume. We take other people's products – their TV shows,

TikTok dances, Instagram reels, video games – and watch or play them. Sometimes we do this for hours a day! We sign up for amusement and diversion in phones, but being imaginative? No thanks.

What if we determined to use our imaginations to serve God in whatever ways he wanted? How would this transform our problems, our relationships, our jobs, or our leisure time? We can make our minds fully available to him, creating white space in our lives and paying attention to our own dreams and ideas that he's put in us.

We don't have to be Albert Einstein, and no one wants us to be. But each of us is called to offer all of our God-given imaginative faculties to him, asking him to enact the creative expressions he wants to bring to the world through us.
To do it, we need to put down our phones.

PRAY:
Father, often we would rather consume than create. We don't know what to create and don't have or want bandwidth to think about it. Forgive us for disregarding the gift you give us in imagination, and excite us with the creativity you share with us. May we be holy makers, as you are. We offer our imaginations to you; anoint them for your purposes. May our phones not distract us from this sacred work.
Amen

REFLECT:
Do you consider yourself an imaginative person? People are imaginative in different ways – cooking, playing music, accounting, gardening, crafting, writing, art, and more. Think of a time in your life when your imagination flowed in a tangible way, and identify the circumstances that allowed this. How does your phone play into your imaginative space (or lack thereof)?

DAY 27 : PLANNING AND STEWARDSHIP ARE KEY PARTS OF A VISION-FUELED LIFE

"The man who had received five bags of gold brought the other five. 'Master,' he said, 'you entrusted me with five bags of gold. See, I have gained five more.' His master replied, 'Well done, good and faithful servant! You have been faithful with a few things; I will put you in charge of many things.'" Matthew 25:20-21

———————————

STEWARDSHIP means taking stock of what we have, and planning ahead to use those things wisely. It's about managing resources with wisdom. It's the opposite of being wasteful.

To be people of vision, we must effectively direct and manage what we have. We can't live the fruitful life that God desires for us, or help extend his kingdom, if we are poor stewards.

Stewardship asks the question, "What have I been given, and what does God want me to do with it?" We look not just at money, as the verse suggests, but also at our time, talent, and possessions. The amount is unimportant, since God is in the business of growing small things offered to him into big things. Our job is simply to identify and offer.

To do this, we must examine the habits that characterize our lives. Our culture teaches us to be over-busy with insignificant things and ignore the more important things. This is what's meant by the "tyranny of the urgent" – we're so busy responding to emails and planning carpool, for example, that we shelve weightier and more significant tasks. Our culture also encourages us to be self-absorbed, fixated on amusement. Phones foster both these: task-masters that keep us hopping, and portals into the recreation that renders us passive.

But our interactions with our phone shouldn't keep us from being good stewards who live with vision. We want to hear "well done, good and faithful servant" when our time on earth is done, and days full of mindless reactivity or endless scrolling will not get us there.

And what about the fact that our phone itself is a resource to be stewarded? We've been given a tool with great capacity to help us live well... if we will only employ wisdom and self-control in the way we use it. Our phones can make us *more* fruitful, not less, if we submit our habits and tendencies to the Holy Spirit and let him direct us.

Let's take seriously the call to submit our lives to God and help him affect this world through us as much as he wants, however he wants. Let's invest our time, talent, and treasure in his kingdom and ask him to grow those investments over time, for his glory. And let's not get sidetracked or derailed by overuse of, and dependence on, our phones.

PRAY:
Father, we are prone to take what we've been given and... sit on it. We tend to be lazy and fearful, and stewarding our lives well feels daunting. Show us where we are selfish or fearful. May we not let our phones lure us into lives of smallness or insignificance. Rather, empower us to grab hold of vision and offer ourselves and everything we have to you as good stewards. Grow our small offerings. Amen

REFLECT:
Which of these do you have the easiest time offering to God: time, talent (your gifts), or treasure (your money)? Which is hardest? Think about how your screen practices enhance your efforts toward living a life of vision and stewardship, and how they detract from doing so. What small adjustments of habit might you make if you want to live more purposefully?

DAY 28 : PARTNERING WITH GOD AROUND THE NOTION OF VISION

"Commit to the Lord whatever you do, and he will establish your plans." Proverbs 16:3

———————————

THERE'S a difference between the way the world uses the word "vision" and the way that God does. For the secular person, vision means "the thing we want to do." For the Jesus-follower, vision most often means "the thing I feel God wants me to do, that he has shown me... and will help me accomplish in his strength."

In Habakkuk 2:2-3, God speaks of a revelation he will soon bring the prophet that he's to write down and broadcast when it comes. God says, "Though it linger, wait for it; it will certainly come and will not delay." Here vision is a combination of receiving input from God about his intentions, and then acting on the input when it arrives. In tandem with God, then, we enact plans to move toward that thing.

In this we see that God has made vision a *collaborative* thing and process. We seek God for input or direction, wait and listen, take what we feel he is saying, and work to execute it. We offer our efforts to him, asking him to help us to steward our actions and resources well. This is what today's proverb gets at when it says "commit to the Lord whatever you do, and he will establish your plans."

All this takes time and intentionality. Living a vision-filled life in collaboration with God doesn't just happen to us as we sit idly by. It's something we're supposed to be doing actively; it is God's call upon our lives.

Our phones often thwart efforts to live with vision. When we enter its orb and start browsing and scrolling, we don't bring a mindset of working collaboratively with God on his larger purposes for our life. Instead we approach our phone as master of our domain, god of our tiny hand-held world. And we get washed away in its distractions, forgetting God and the big picture of his world and ways. The phone reinforces these mindsets.

It is possible to commit ourselves and our actions to the Lord in our phone use, and to have our phone time complement (instead of work against) the vision-filled life to which God has called us. Self-control and a surrendered spirit *can* pave the way for God to create a phone-use ethos that pleases him and poses no obstacle to a partnership-based life.

Let's lean in!

_____

PRAY:
Holy Spirit, you are counselor, comforter, and friend, and you show us which way you want us to go. Thank you that we can rely on you to lead and direct us as we look to you. We can collaborate with you in living a life of impact, expanding the kingdom of God! May we prefer the hope-filled vision you give, as we ask and wait, to the stagnation of a phone-filled life. And may we honor you in all we do.
Amen

REFLECT:
How do you respond to the truth that God uses us, that he cares about our plans, and that he wants to collaborate with us to bring new things into this world? How does this idea of "collaborating with God" sit with you? Think about how your phone use can distract or detract from living on mission for (and with) God. Is this the case for you?

A WAY FORWARD:

Phone use for the God-minded

DAYS 29 — 30

———

DAY 29 : THE CRITICAL ROLE OF SELF-CONTROL – FOR FAITH AND PHONE USE

God's grace "teaches us to say 'no' to ungodliness and worldly passions, and to live self-controlled, upright, and godly lives in this present age." (Titus 2:11)

_____

THE irony of our phone is that in order to use it well, we must harness and employ large amounts of self-control. And yet, research clearly shows that using the device *erodes* self-control. The engineers who make our phones and their apps exploit human psychology to intentionally make them addictive.

We are, as has been said, at war. The trick is to realize the battled being waged against us... and fight.

For God's people to live well in the modern day, we must be as "shrewd as serpents and innocent as doves" (Matt. 10:16)... and this means with our devices. We start by acknowledging and assessing the ways that overuse of phones is harming us and interfering with our relationship with God. We first do a reckoning; then we prepare ourselves for attack.

This raises the question of *how* to attack. We know that self-control is a fruit of the spirit (Gal. 5:23) – mandatory, not optional – but practically speaking, how do we get it?

Since God calls us to be people of self-control, he will grow it in us through the Holy Spirit as we ask him for it.[25] So a first step is to intentionally commit our way to him in our daily habits, ask him to alert us when we face temptation, and pray for increased self-control.

The next step is to make adjustments to our daily habits. Andy Crouch refers to these adjustments as nudges and offers this wise observation about their importance:

> "We are continually being nudged by our devices toward a set of choices. The question is whether those choices are leading us to the life we actually want. I want a life of conversation and friendship, not distraction and entertainment; but every day, many times a day, I'm nudged in the wrong direction. One key part of the art of living fearfully with technology is setting up better nudges for ourselves."[26]

There are many practical resources that can help you assess and re-establish your nudges. I've developed a simple, step-by-step guide for exactly this reason, *Reset: 21 Days to a New Relationship with Your Phone*, and I provide other offerings at www.susanbarico.com. Many other excellent authors, such as those quoted in this book, offer resources as well. Pray that God will lead you to the path that's best for you, and then do some research.

Let's keep our eyes on the goal and remember why all this matters: greater self-control in phone use helps us better be the people God wants, and live the life he calls us to.

PRAY:
God, we are often undisciplined, lazy, and self-consumed...
and worse, we don't even care. Forgive us for loving ourselves,
comfort, and entertainment more than you. Counselor and
Encourager, give us the self-control we need so we may use our
phones in ways that please you.
Amen

REFLECT:
Would you characterize yourself as a disciplined or undisciplined
person? Scan your life and normal routines. What circumstances
allow you to be most self-controlled with your phone? Have you
set up any nudges that help you use your phone optimally?

DAY 30 : BALANCE (AND THE TRAP OF LEGALISM) IN PHONE USE

"Now the Lord is the Spirit, and where the Spirit of the Lord is, there is freedom." 2 Corinthians 3:17

———————————

PEOPLE look at the subject of phone use much like they look at junk food: they don't want to talk about it. It's a topic that causes guilt. We know we should engage less and aren't proud of our tendencies or actions, so we just sidestep the issue. We don't deny so much as avoid.

This is not helpful.

God is not a God of condemnation, and he wants us to live in truth and light. Also, he's the giver of good gifts – including chocolate cake, potato chips... and our phones! He is the *author*, not killer, of our delight.

The reason Jesus so often spoke against legalism is because people take God's good words and commands and warp them, making them condemning. The spirit of legalism wants to make everything heavy and everyone feel inadequate. The currency of legalism is guilt and shame... but the God who loves us has life and freedom for us![27] And he sets us free from the trap of legalism every chance he gets.

So let's end by remembering: your phone is a good gift from God. Using it is not innately sinful. Even using it for many hours a day is not a sin, depending on the app and context. (For example, an audiobook or catch-up call with a friend can eat up hours... yet is fruitful!) Let's kick unnecessary guilt and shame to the curb.

We honor God as we offer our phones to him, daily and hourly, and ask him to guide the ways we use them. We pray that we would keep him and his ways before us, as first in our minds... and that we would be people of right presence, attention, solitude, connection, rest, contentment, and vision. That these things would be anchored in him and come *first*, and ever be a filter through which we gauge our technology use.

We can trust God to answer our prayers. He will help us honor him as we use our phones... and he will use us, as we do so, in simple but powerful ways.

What a God we serve! Here's to freedom – and to flourishing as humans as we follow him.

————————

PRAY:
Lord God, it is so difficult to walk the line between caring too little and caring too much. While we want to be people of self-control, we would not be legalists – nor would we pursue paths that increase guilt or shame. Help us walk this line well. Let us use our phones in ways that honor you, in a right spirit of freedom.
Amen

REFLECT:
Think back over the seven phone themes we've looked at these thirty days – presence, attention, solitude, connection, rest, contentment, and vision. Which area presents the biggest stronghold for you in your phone use? Pray into it. In which areas do you feel that, by the grace of God, you're growing?

NOTES

[1] Ed Cyzewksi, *Reconnect: Spiritual Restoration from Digital Distraction,* Herald Press, 2020, 23

[2] See 2 Corinthians 10:5, "we take captive every thought to make it obedient to Christ."

[3] Wendy Speake, *The 40-Day Social Media Fast* (Grand Rapids: Baker Books, 2020), 70

[4] Brother Lawrence, *The Practice of the Presence of God*, (Martino Fine Books, 2016), 29.

[5] "How Your Attention Has Become the Biggest Commodity," Mindful.org, accessed January 31, 2022. https://www.mindful.org/attention-become-biggest-commodity/

[6] John Mark Comer, *The Ruthless Elimination of Hurry: How to Stay Emotionally Healthy and Spiritually Alive in the Chaos of the Modern World* (Colorado Springs: Waterbrook Press, 2019), 39.

[7] John Eldredge speaks of this in episode 210 of Annie F. Downs' "That Sounds Fun" podcast, https://www.anniefdowns.com/podcast/episode-210-john-eldredge/

[8] Cal Newport, *Digital Minimalism, Choosing a Focused Life in a Noisy World* (New York: Portfolio/Penguin, 2019), 103

[9] Henri Nouwen, *The Way of the Heart* (The Seabury Press: Canada, 1981), 15

[10] Sherry Turkle, *Reclaiming Conversation: The Power of Talk in a Digital Age* (New York: Penguin Random House, 2015), 172

[11] "Like: a documentary about finding balance in our digital world." https://www.indieflix.com/like

[12] Tony Reinke, *12 Ways Your Phone is Changing You* (Wheaton: Crossway, 2017), 75

[13] Ibid, 77

[14] Merriam Webster definition of "encourage," accessed January 31, 2022, https://www.merriam-webster.com/dictionary/encourage

[15] Catherine Price, *How to Break Up With Your Phone* (California, New York: Ten Speed Press, 2018), 142

[16] Ibid

[17] Wendy Speake, *The 40-Day Social Media Fast* (Grand Rapids: Baker Books, 2020), 44

[18] Cal Newport, *Digital Minimalism, Choosing a Focused Life in a Noisy World* (New York: Portfolio/Penguin, 2019), 44

[19] "Giving Thanks Can Make You Happier," Harvard Health Publishing, accessed January 25, 2020, https://www.health.harvard.edu/health-beat/giving-thanks-can-make-you-happier

ABOUT THE AUTHOR

Susan B. Arico is a digital wellness expert and writer on screen related topics, primarily how cell phone use affects our souls (#cellandsoul). She's the creator of the digital detox guide *Reset: 21 Days to a New Relationship with Your Phone.* Her essays have appeared in *Today's Christian Woman, WomenLeaders.com, Joyful Life Magazine, For Every Mom, The Mighty, Everyday Matters Bible for Women: Practical Encouragement to Make Every Day Matter*, and elsewhere. Susan is also a strategy consultant to large nonprofits; in both her consulting and writing projects she works to advance human flourishing. She lives in a 1690 house on three New England acres with her husband, four children, dog, and twelve chickens. Connect with her online at www.susanbarico.com and on Instagram @susanbarico.